JRCC Bookstore & Library
416 . 222-7105 ext. **221**
www.jrcc.org/bookstore

THE ABRAHAM PRINCIPLE

Where Faith and Science Meet

Dr. Arnie Gotfryd, PhD

The Abraham Principle

Copyright © 2014 by Dr. Arnie Gotfryd, PhD

All rights reserved. No part of this book may be reproduced or transmitted in any form or by any means without written permission of the author.

Contact: arnie@maximind.ca or 1-416-858-9868

ISBN 978-0-9878494-1-0

Cover Design: Virtually Possible Designs
Eclipse Photography: Stefan Seip – astromeeting.de

This book is dedicated to the Lubavitcher Rebbe,
Rabbi Menachem Mendel Schneerson,
an individual who, from among all men, best represents
the wisdom, courage, love and leadership that
the Patriarch Abraham embodied.

Like Abraham, the Rebbe's passion and purpose is for
universal wellness and sustainability, a world united
in goodness and kindness under one G-d.

Acknowledgments

This book has been incubating in the back of my mind for about 30 years. It would have stayed there indefinitely were it not for the help of some people near and dear to me.

First, my wife Leah who really assisted in many ways: She's an insightful, gentle, yet firm critic with a gift for editing the written word. She has always been patient with my passion for exploring the interplay of science and faith, even though (a) by nature, the closest she'd get to science is Captain Kirk, and (b) there were many more practical things she would have rather had me do.

Rabbi Yosaif Yarmush, a great friend and mentor, when I was stuck trying to decide between blogging or booking years ago, pushed me toward regular articles, saying that when the time will come, your articles can be turned into book. Thanks to his sage advice, my articles reached tens of thousands and voilà! Here is the first book to grow out of those.

Next is Rabbi Simon Jacobson, who, at a turning point in my life, advised me that in choosing what to do next, I should think as big as I can, and then when reconsidering my choices, think bigger yet. May he be blessed in doing the same.

I am grateful to the Lubavitcher Rebbe for spending time with me, for showing me how to discover G-d through science, for elucidating for me and for all of us how causal reasoning underlies not only modern science but traditional faith as well, and for understanding my soul and for directing me in how to fulfill its mission in the world. May this book be counted as a step towards that fulfillment.

Finally, I would like to thank the Creator and Sustainer of all for allowing Abraham's life and teachings to take root in this world and flourish to the point where his most cherished aspiration for the world may in fact become fully and imminently realized – mankind united under one G-d in a world of goodness and kindness.

Table of Contents

Legends Old and New 1

A Theory of Everything 9

So Far Out, It's In 19

Something From Nothing 27

Hide and Seek 33

G-d is a Verb 37

Walking the Talk 43

Give and Take 49

Knowing and Caring 53

Beauty, Meet Truth 57

The "Why" Chromosome 67

The Power of One 71

What is Life? 75

Faith and Physics: A Story 83

Legends Old and New

Abraham. Ibrahim. Avraham. It's a name that carries much weight in the world, perhaps more than any other. Nearly four billion of the world's seven billion inhabitants belong to one of the world's major "Abrahamic" religions.

What makes them Abrahamic is their identification with ethical monotheism, belief in a Supreme Being, a Creator, who is involved in the world and cares about its people. About three quarters of the world's nearly two hundred nations are dominated by religions that claim a spiritual heritage that traces back to one man – Abraham.

Indeed his Hebrew name, Avraham, means father of many nations. But for all his fame, who was he really? Our earliest stories of Abraham come from the book of Genesis, but those tales reveal nothing of why he, of all people, should be so widely considered the father of ethical monotheism. After all, Noah preceded Abraham by many generations and Adam was earlier still. Nonetheless, it is specifically Abraham who is branded the patriarch. Why?

What exactly did he innovate? How did he come up with his ideas? How was he received in his times? And how do we know? And what relevance could any of this have for our ultramodern, hi-tech, multicultural world?

The key to all this is encoded in ancient rabbinic sources called Midrash that chronicle legends over thousands of years. Some of these sources are available in English.

According to the Midrash, Abraham was born in 1812 BCE in the ancient Mesopotamian town of Ur Kasdim. As a young child in a pagan culture, he practiced idolatry and prayed to the sun, believing it to have created the heavens and the earth. But something didn't quite click.

Whenever the sun set, it was out of the picture and the moon and stars dominated the night sky. Realizing the sun's limitations he prayed to the moon. With time he realized that neither is the ultimate answer. He came to the conclusion that there must be one invisible Creator with unlimited power and knowledge.

Abraham was absolutely convinced that the prevailing pagan beliefs were wrong. He set about sharing his findings with everyone he met and successfully persuaded thousands to drop paganism in favor of his "heretical" views. Although popular with the public, Abraham was spurned by both family and the ruling class for bucking the system.

After narrowly escaping martyrdom for refusing to deify the emperor, Abraham was forced to flee Babylon and took refuge in a reclusive monastery where he studied theology and kabbalah with a few other marginalized monotheists, descendants of Noah. Abraham went on to author the famed Book of Formation, Sefer Yetzirah in Hebrew, the earliest known book on kabbalah.

Only after all this does Genesis pick up the plot with Abraham's call to the Promised Land and the subsequent history of his descendants, both Jews and Gentiles.

But questions remain, and perhaps the biggest one is – who cares? It's just history, right? Wrong.

This much-overlooked legend has encoded within it a profound philosophical principle. It is a principle which provides the key to modern science. Its conceptual core underlies quantum physics, cosmology, ecology, and information technology. But there is much more to it.

This principle has the power to unlock human potential, raise confidence, optimize wellness, harmonize relationships, advance prosperity, remove anxiety and fear, and generate peace of mind. It will even bring about sustainability and world peace.

Are these claims not overly bold, even outlandish? Definitely. But are they accurate? Over the course of this book and its sequel, "The Soul of Science," the reader is invited to judge for himself.

Two stories

A Lubavitcher Chassid meets up with a radical Muslim on a subway car and they get into a conversation.

If you think this is a joke, think again. This happened to my wife and me a few years ago, ironically, while on our way to a huge multi-cultural event. The gala dinner that night was co-sponsored by the Canadian League for Human Rights and it was in honor of a Jew and a Sikh for their joint humanitarian philanthropy.

We were sitting on the subway, chatting, when a young man took up a position in the aisle directly in front of us, holding an exceptionally well-worn copy of "Hezbollah: Party of God." At eighteen inches, I was uniquely situated to appreciate the intimate relationship that probably existed between the Mediterranean looking youth before me and the graying, dog-eared, spine-crumbled manifesto cradled in his hand. A chill went up my spine.

As I looked up, his eyes met mine and our gazes locked. I spoke first, not quietly, but not loud. "It's one G-d for the whole world, right?"

Surprised, he hesitated, "…Yeah."

I went on, "He wants, goodness and kindness. Right?"

His gaze shifted, he glanced at me again, and then away, "…Yeah."

Feeling hopeful, I extended my hand. "Let's shake on it."

"I cannot do that," he said, as he turned a bit away.

"Only what we agree on," and then I counted out the three points on my fingers. "G-d, goodness, and kindness. Nothing else."

"I gotta think about it." He turned and walked off. My heart was thumping. I tried not to look his way although my mind was on his jacket – was there a bulge around the waist? A few minutes later, he returned. "I thought about it …Okay."

Pleased, I offered my hand again. This time he took it, and we shook – almost held – hands for a good long while. In my fifty-odd years I've shaken a lot of hands. I've had limp fish handshakes, bone crusher handshakes, perfunctory up-down roboticals, and mazal-tov-reception-liners. This was different. I felt love. It felt like something between a long-lost relative and an estranged son coming back home. We let go and he walked away. A few minutes later, he was back again, just as the train was slowing down.

"Good evening sir, good evening madam" he said. The train stopped, and he was gone.

To me, this is what Moshiach Now is all about. G-d, goodness, kindness, people united, a better world. Is it that simple? Maybe.

Another story.

Vladimir Putin is no great friend of Israel today. Yet his respect for Judaism, especially in its most pristine form is well-known. He's an admirer of Chabad and since assuming office has restored countless properties that were confiscated by the Soviets, and returned them to Jewish communities across the country. How did this tough, ultrapatriotic, ex-KGB boss become so friendly with Jewish orthodoxy?

The inside story was revealed by Russian Chief Rabbi, Berl Lazar at the inaugural Chabad-Israeli dinner in Toronto some years back. He told us that he and President Putin presided together at the opening day ceremony for the Jewish Community Center in Moscow. As the event drew to a close, Putin said to Lazar, "Let's say L'Chaim!" Lazar said, "Fine, but better inside."

Some vodka and condiments were quickly set up but the President wanted something more. "Do you have any gefilte fish?" he asked. You can imagine it didn't take long to serve that familiar delicacy, but again the distinguished guest wasn't satisfied. "This isn't real gefilte fish. I know what real gefilte fish tastes like." And he proceeded to tell R' Lazar a story from his childhood.

Little Vladimir usually came home from primary school to an empty house because both parents were off working. He'd run around the apartment block, getting into all kinds of mischief as energetic, unsupervised little boys are wont to do. The neighbors didn't take kindly to his pranks and let him know it in no uncertain terms.

One family in the building was different. The elderly Jewish couple would call him in, offer him something to eat, and tell him what a good boy he was. They made an indelible impression on the President-to-be, the husband with his skull-cap and bushy beard and the wife with her delicious cooking, especially the gefilte fish! He especially liked the pleasant and dignified way they spoke to each other.

From that time, he liked and respected religious Jews, and when he became President he vowed to himself to help them in any way he can.

G-d, goodness, kindness. Maybe it is that simple.

Abraham's values at work.

A Theory of Everything

It's official. The most powerful concept in world history was developed by a child thinking deeply about food. Yes, he was Jewish. And no, it did not have to do with his mother.

Plurality

What is the Abraham Principle?

What concept did that venerable sage actually innovate? And how did he figure it out?

The most authoritative information I could find about all this comes from what one might call family records – ancient and mediaeval rabbinic sources like the Midrash HaGadol, the Midrash Rabba, the Talmud and Maimonides all referring us back to the year 1948. (No, not that 1948. You are thinking of the year that the modern State called Israel was formed. I mean the year that the Patriarch Abraham was born according to the Jewish calendar, 1948 years from Creation, some 3800 years ago.)

There it explains how Abraham since his earliest childhood was an exceptionally inquisitive and independent thinker obsessed with trying to figure out why things were the way they were. Of course kids tend to be that way in any case and Abraham was neither the first nor the last. But he was unique in how far he would push the logic.

His context was pagan. His parents were pagan, his neighbors were pagan. In fact paganism was the only religious expression in the Mesopotamian culture that he was born into. What this means is that they believed in many gods – a whole collection of separate powers each guiding its own part of the natural world.

People were not stupid. They realized they were powerless against the forces of nature and that there is more to life than meets the eye. They also realized that these forces can oppose and conflict with each other or they could also be independent of each other. What they did not realize was the unity behind the forces of nature. So when they wanted rain, they prayed to a rain god. When they wanted to be blessed with children, they prayed to a fertility goddess.

By the way, people today think they are smart because they believe in one whereas others believe in many. But if you stop to think about it, what do we do if the One G-d says to do something we don't want to do. We say to ourselves, "Well… there are more important things than what He wants right now." So now there is a greater reason than G-d for doing this or that? Aren't we making that reason into a G-d?

Ever heard of the Almighty Dollar? And that's in addition to all the official religions that practice one form or another of pagan worship.

The way Chabad.org summarizes the Midrash, it tells us that "Abraham started with this question: Why should we bow down to idols, gods that we ourselves make? We should bow to the earth, for it produces crops that sustain us. Therefore, he began to worship the earth."

Of course he didn't stop there, but I'd like to dwell on this stage of his thinking, just for a moment. Would you have thought of doing that if you lived back then? Everybody's doing the socially acceptable thing because that's the way you do it. Don't ask questions. Just accept it. Does this sound familiar? How free are kids today to question the wisdom of their parents, their teachers, their culture? I wonder.

I think it was a pretty smart cognitive leap for a three-year-old. You eat food. Where does it come from? For those of you who think it grows in Aisle 3 in the grocery store, I'll tell you: It grows from the ground. So why pray to some statue you made yesterday when the ground that gives or doesn't give its bounty has been sitting around forever. If there is a spiritual force behind that, let's talk, the child thought. I want dinner tomorrow. I'm not interested in a drought or a crop failure. If I'm going to say please and thank you, I'm going to do that to the right being. So he prayed – whoops, to the earth – but he prayed.

But this leaves us with a question. Why should anyone imagine that the earth knows anything at all about our needs? Why should one imagine that it hears prayer? Or that it controls one's destiny? It's just dumb dirt, right? One would normally be tempted to just write this off to pagan foolishness, but the fact that Abraham himself took this step in life (albeit as a child), and that it's recorded in the Midrash as part of Torah proves that there is a lesson in it for us.

It seems to me that the lesson is that Abraham understood that there has to be consciousness somewhere involved in the earth/food/human ecosystem. How so? There are three things here, none of them conscious of how food from the ground sustains a human. Carrots don't know me. I don't understand them. But there has to be consciousness of what the carrot can do for me as well as what I can get from it somewhere. Otherwise how else could a dumb carrot do such a sophisticated job as sustain a human's life?

It made sense to Abraham at the time that the common factor is the earth. I need the earth. Carrots need the earth. It's big, it's everywhere and everything is connected with it. Voila! The conscious powerful beneficient being is the earth! Okay, so it's wrong, but a good try nonetheless.

Now back to the story. "Then he saw that the earth needs rain, and began to worship the sky." This is deep. He sees the earth is not in control of its own food-giving ability. It depends on some external factor, rain, and that comes down from the sky. If the sky is the source of the rains then the sky is ultimately in charge of whether I eat and therefore whether I do or do not live. Besides, it's bigger. Much, much bigger. But a thinking person realizes that the sky is not the be all and end all either. What good would the sky be for sustaining life without the sun?

"Later, he saw that the most brilliant creation in the sky was the sun, and began to worship it. Afterwards, when the sun set and the moon rose, he began to worship the moon. When the sun rose the next morning, he did not know what to do. He did not see which was stronger: the sun or the moon. So Abraham continued in a quandary, questioning what was the true G-d."

So much for the Midrash.

Let's step back and look at Abraham's quest as a logical problem. By this time the question was larger than who's taking care of dinner. He realized that just like he needs his lackings filled so does everything else. By now he was seeking some entity capable of creating and sustaining the world as a whole. With nothing more than the world itself to go by, he had to work by inference.

Knowing that everything that happens, happens for a reason, Abraham set out to discover that reason. Put another way, he set out to explore what it is that's responsible for the existence of… well, you name it: Matter, energy, motion, and life on the grandest scale imaginable. A theory of everything, if you will.

No wonder, then, that he tried worshipping the sun. It is huge, powerful, and immensely influential. It is our preeminent source of light and heat. It drives the hydrological cycle and makes the plants grow and the animals thrive. It sets the days and seasons.

Today, we can overlook the sun. There are countless thousands of people who wake up indoors, take elevators down to subways, commute to skyscrapers they access from underground, and return home at the end of the day after shopping, dining and taking in a show, all without stepping outside. But back then, who knows, in a Middle

Eastern Bronze Age society, it was probably a no brainer to imagine the sun as the creator of all.

But the sun has its limits. The moon rules the night. Tides, biorhythms and moods are all heavily linked to lunar cycles. Recent studies have even shown that the frequency with which animals bite humans is closely linked to the phases of the moon. And if the moon can act where the sun cannot, it shows a certain greatness above and beyond the sun itself. So Abraham worshipped the moon.

Now he could have stopped right there, like the rest of his compatriots. Each heavenly body with its own sphere of influence. Radiate and reflect, give and take, positive and negative, masculine and feminine, duality works fine for many cultures and faiths. But not for Abraham. He recognized duality, yet he suspected an underlying unity. But why?

Unity

The sun and the moon have a special relationship. While different as night and day (in light, in heat, in motion, in phases, and in seasons), they nevertheless share two remarkable qualities. First, they are exactly the same angular (or apparent) size, even though the sun is huge and far and the moon is small and close. Second, their paths intersect every once in a while resulting in spectacular eclipses. Whoever has witnessed a total solar eclipse knows the awe and wonder this majestic event evokes. It was obvious to Abraham that the coordination of the sun and the moon was not a mere chance phenomenon.

Abraham understood that most basic principle of human logic that everything that happens, happens for a reason. The very fact that solar and lunar sizes and motions are coordinated is itself a something, albeit an abstract something, which requires an explanation. The sun and moon should be viewed as an orderly system with a suitable cause.

Now the question was, what could the cause of this systemic property be? Could the two-part, sun-moon system originate in a duality or other plurality, say pantheon, of forces? Remember that Abraham had no clue about monotheism at the time. He addressed his question first using the pagan cognitive tools that were his heritage.

Well, he probably thought, if it were the case that some divine plurality created the system, what was coordinating the parts of that higher plurality? And if nothing was coordinating the higher plurality, then how did their coordination come to be? Abraham wasn't ready to drop cause and effect. Ascribing the natural system to a supernatural system only pushes off the coordination issue. Abraham concluded that there had to be ultimately one factor unifying the sun-moon system. But what was it?

Beyond Within

What could be coordinating the sun-moon system?

One possibility was that the control was within the system. That would mean, in effect, that the sun and the moon were coordinating themselves. But that did not seem feasible because seeing their individual orbits and properties, it was clear that the sun was not controlling the moon and the moon was not controlling the sun. Therefore the control must be some factor which is not the sun and not the moon. Perhaps it was the earth, but that could not be because the earth was itself integrated systematically with the sun and the moon, for after all, that's why Abraham worshipped them originally. The stars and planets too had their regular, integrated motions and specific roles in the grand scheme of things, so they were not the organizing force.

Clearly, whatever that force or being was, had to have two properties. It had to be external to the parts of the system, and it had to be more powerful than them, to keep all the parts in systemic order. Given that the system under consideration was now not just the sun and the moon but indeed the heavens and the earth as a whole, being external to it all implied being transcendent, and being more powerful than it all meant being omnipotent.

So now Abraham was looking beyond the system for a transcendent, omnipotent force responsible for creating and managing the entire physical universe. Okay, you may think, problem solved, odyssey over, monotheism established. . . or is it? Abraham might not have jumped to the One G-d idea quite yet. But "Why not?" you may ask. "How many transcendent, omnipotent beings are there?"

So Far Out, It's In

What started off as a child's inquiry into "who's in charge of the food around here?" morphed into a lifelong passion about "how does the world work and why?"

These days such questions are still being asked and the two major ways of dealing with them boil down to Science or Religion. In the minds of most, Science and Religion mainly disagree but truth be told, that's old-think. New think is more about synergy.

That's why Abraham's logic is more relevant today than ever. He analyzed systems, breaking them down into component parts and also viewed them as a whole greater than the sum of the parts. The analytical part is called reductionism and that's the hallmark of 19th Century science. The system view is called holism and that's the ever-increasing scientific style of 21stCentury.

Hearkening back to our patriarch's mental odyssey in the previous chapter, we followed his reasoning to the point where the system under question was the universe as a whole. What he came to understand, and now we understand it too, is that the force beyond the universe has to be above it all (transcendent), aware of it all (omniscient), and in control of it all (omnipotent) as well.

Transcendence

One of the qualities that Abraham ascribed to the One Above is at once the very best and the very worst. It is the best because it has the greatest explanatory power. And it is also the worst, because it poses major marketing challenges.

That property is transcendence. What does this mean? It means above and beyond, but beyond its spatial connotation it means abstraction. Ultimately, abstraction means no space, no time, no body, and no parts.

But how do you communicate an idea like that to your average Joe? Nothing to see, smell, taste, touch or hear. An imperceptible ultimate force. But even that would not have been so bad as long as people could imagine someplace in heaven where this entity could reside, and some kind of form, albeit abstract, that this entity could have. But Abraham did away with all that, and not on a whim, either. In a word, the ultimate being had to be abstracted from any notion of space and form, physical or spiritual.

To exemplify, let's consider the popular notion that the Creator resides in heaven. Sounds fair. People live on earth and the Big Guy lives in heaven. Isn't that what most people think? But what and where is heaven, and what does it mean that He lives there? If they told you "Take a Voyager Taxi to Alpha Centauri, turn left and it's right beside Andromeda, you can't miss it, just ask for the Boss and tell him I sent you" I don't think you would buy it.

With a little more abstraction, we could call heaven a higher world and say the Creator lives there because He is spiritual and not physical. Well, that would be a little better because at least it shifts the discussion above the physical plane. But still, it relegates the Creator to a place, a spiritual place but a place nonetheless, so Abraham had to accept that the Creator transcends spiritual "space" just as He transcends physical space.

Now how about time? Time is a creation as well; it's part of the space-time continuum, and Abraham figured this out too. If everything has one source and time is part of everything then that one source created time too. Abraham had never heard of Genesis because Moses hadn't written about it yet, and he had not yet met any other monotheists, but still, he deduced that there had to be a beginning and that the true Source had to "precede" that beginning. The Creator had to be beyond time just as He/She/It had to be beyond space.

What does it mean to be beyond time and space? It sounds absurd. "Outside" is a spatial concept. To be outside of space makes no sense. Similarly, "before" is a temporal concept. To be before time makes no sense either. But the fact that human reason cannot quite digest the conclusion does not mean that the reasoning is faulty.

On the contrary, it reflects the greatness of the idea that it cannot be grasped by the logic that conceived it.

Immanence

Abraham's cognitive quest took him to the great beyond, indeed the ultimate beyond.

The ultimate beyond. What an expression. In a way it's scary, wild, yet attractive, mysterious. But we need not let go of our rational faculties, at least not yet, because the Abraham Principle is a logical notion and we have yet to exhaust its rational implications.

We have said that transcendence is about being above and beyond, being abstracted from any limitation. But is that not also a sort of limitation?

So Far Out, It's In

To explain, imagine you've got some unlimited being and you have to figure out where to put it. If you place it within the world and not beyond it, you have definitely limited it, so that's not the right placement. If you put it beyond the world and not within it, you have limited it in a different way, by being beyond and not within.

To be truly unlimited means that beyond and within are equal in relation to it. Ultimately, to be beyond beyond must include to be within.

So here we have a Being, an ultimate being, that is not only beyond the world but within it too. Not only beyond space but within its confines; not only before time but in time as well.

But wait a moment, you might say. Weren't we looking for an explanation of space and time? An explanation that was beyond the parts, beyond the system, transcendent? So what are we doing coming full circle, looking for the Creator within space and time? Isn't that what Abraham was rebelling against in the first place?

Good question. And in good Jewish style, we will answer this question with another question... the famous "Are we or aren't we?" paradox.

Once the patriarch Abraham realized that the Prime Mover was had to be just as much in the world as beyond it, he was faced with the very same dilemma that has plagued philosophers ever since: The Are We or Aren't We Paradox.

Simply stated it amounts to this: If G-d exists, he must be infinite. That's Monotheism 101, no way around it. Being that He's infinite, there is no place devoid of Him, that is, He must be omnipresent, He exists everywhere. So if there is no place where He isn't, He must be here where I am. Because if He is not here where I am, He is limited spatially, and if He's limited in space, He's not unlimited and therefore He's not G-d. So He must be here where I am. The only problem is, I'm here and I'm not Him. And if it's really Him that's here and not me, then what am I doing here? Do I really exist? What's going on here?

To understand this better, there is a famous story about a Chassidic charity collector who traveled to a Jewish community that was not friendly to the Chassidic movement. So anti-Chassidic were they, that they appointed a community leader to interrogate visiting charity collectors to ensure they weren't members of "The Sect" as those townsfolk not-too-lovingly referred to the Chassidic movement.

So this erstwhile Chassidic alms-gatherer was being pointedly questioned by the community leader, saying "What is your opinion of the Sect?"

The collector replied, "Oh them. They are always thinking about themselves whereas the fine people of this town are always thinking about G-d!" Satisfied with this answer, he was given a note of endorsement to support him in his rounds. Once he had finished is work in town, he stopped by the local synagogue to bid farewell to the congregants.

He walked up to the lectern, gave it a bang and announced: "Gentlemen! Some of you may have been wondering what I meant when I said that the Chassidim are always thinking about themselves whereas the people of this fine town are always thinking about G-d. What I meant was this: What is reality? You are probably thinking 'what a silly question'. Reality is what you see all around you. So for you, the fact that you are real is obvious. So you will always be wondering about the Creator, asking yourself how could it be that He is here when the fact is that you are here and not Him? The Chassidim however, realize that G-d is the true reality, so they are always wondering about themselves, thinking how can they be here, when the fact is that G-d is really here, and not them!"

With that he dashed out the door into the waiting wagon and sped off down the road before they had a chance to react to their lesson in philosophy.

And so, dear reader, there is no way around it. All of existence is a paradox, and we live in an enigmatic universe. And with regards to whether and how one might come to resolve the Are We or Aren't We Paradox, that's a topic for next chapter.

Something from Nothing

Scientists speak of "The Field," an indivisible wholeness beyond space and time that is the ultimate ground of reality. Does this sound familiar? Another thinker, long ago, got there first.

Let's rewind the cosmos back to the beginning, and then just a little bit more, to get an inkling of how to resolve the Are We or Aren't We paradox.

Choose your beginning.

Many people believe in a big bang creation, a "singularity" that started the universe with an immensely powerful infusion of primordial light in the distant past. Others believe in a six day creation that started the universe with an immensely powerful infusion of primordial light in the distant past.

In either case there was a beginning to the physical universe, a beginning to time and space, a first event that emerged from absolute nothingness. But how could that be? How could something come from nothing?

Thirty-eight hundred years ago, Abraham had not heard of a six-day creation. He also hadn't heard of the big bang.

But he did figure out using causal reasoning that there must have been a beginning. (Even if, for argument's sake, time were infinite or cyclic, in which case it would have neither beginning nor end, the cycle as a whole would still be subject to causality.)

In any case, from observing and contemplating nature, Abraham deduced a number of things, including that the universe did not make itself and that prior to the first defining moment of creation, there had to be an undefined Creator. He also reasoned that this Creator could not be a thing. In fact the most cogent thing one might say about this Creator is that He is the consummate example of no-thing-ness.

But wait a moment. What's the difference between saying that the Creator is no-thing and saying that the Creator is nothing? We are basically using the same terms to define monotheism and atheism! But these are obviously not the same, for in one scenario, the world and everything that's in it is an exquisitely planned and executed masterpiece while in the other it's a collosal, uncaused, accidental, cosmic hiccup (without a hiccuper, no less!)

Abraham knew the difference between no-thing-ness and nothingness. He empathized with those who felt that they are real and the Creator is zero. Yet he knew that actually he was the zero while the Creator is the Real One, strange as that might be.

It's all a matter of perspective. From the Divine perspective, we are like the creatures in our dreams, vivid, yet ephemeral, constantly subject to the creative imagination of the dreamer. Were G-d to remove His mind from us, we would vanish.

The difference however is that our dreams and imagination can only conjure up *images* of reality. G-d's imagining makes a *real* world! Now that's a trick. The No-Thing which is the true Something makes a something which is really a nothing but is nonetheless a Divine creation and therefore is Real!

The no-thing-ness that precedes creation is the great divide, the Big Block, the curtain that hides the Divine presence from the Creations. That curtain allows us free choice, allows evil to exist, allows us to relate to G-d, and Him to us. It allows the created to seek the Creator in an ultimate game of hide-and-go-seek, and it provides a context for reward once the game is up.

The Looking Glass

The curtain dividing Divine and human perspectives operates like a one-way mirror, or like the tinted glass on some automobile windows. The Creator sees us up close and personal, but no one looking back can see in.

As a result, human knowledge and Divine knowledge are utterly different. When I come to know something, that knowledge adds to me incrementally. There is me, the thing outside of me, and my knowledge of it. Three separate things.

When G-d knows something, He doesn't change. He, His knowledge, and what He knows are all one thing. And His knowledge adds nothing to Him, because He knows things by knowing Himself.

To explain, there is a story that's told about the famous Alter Rebbe, author of the classic chassidic text, the Tanya, who traveled to console the family of a colleague who had passed away. One of the children, then aged six, who later became the saintly Yisrael of Ruzhin, posed a question to the Alter Rebbe, as follows.

"The verse states, 'Hear O Israel, the L-rd is G-d, the L-rd is One.' If so, there is nothing else but G-d. The next verse says 'You should love the L-rd your G-d with all your heart, with all your soul, and with all your might.' What is going on here? Is G-d telling G-d to love G-d?"

The Alter Rebbe, who was noted for short explanations at that time in his life, gave the child a lengthy explanation of some two hours. The gist of his explanation was based on the fact that when a Jew says this prayer, he interjects a third verse between these two. That verse emphasizes the kingship of G-d, and the consequent gulf between the king and the people. Having effected such a separation, it then becomes possible to love G-d.

Not all of us today are as spiritually attuned as that six-year-old, but we are all able to achieve a somewhat elevated consciousness. By meditating on the one-way mirror, we discover that the great divide that separates us, unites us even more.

(Further reading - Likutei Torah, Devarim. Maimonides, Laws of Torah Foundations 2:10, esp. English commentary, Moznaim ed. p.174)

Hide and Seek

The key to the Are We or Aren't We Paradox is tzimtzum, the "curtain" that separates the human perspective from the Divine. But why is that important?

G-d doesn't want robots.

If He did, He wouldn't have hidden so well from His creations. But hide He did, so now we are busy trying to peer behind the veil, to discover the ultimate, to transcend, to awaken.

Or not. Sometimes we are busy with other things and the veil is just a veil, soon forgotten.

The story is told of a rebbe who found a child crying and asked him what's wrong. "I've been playing hide-and-go-seek and I was hiding but my friends stopped looking for me and went away." The rebbe cast his eyes heavenward and said, "Master of the Universe. Your children have been looking for you so long and you have hidden so well, that they have stopped looking for you. Come out of hiding and return to your children!"

Abraham knew that Divine concealment has a purpose. Without it, there could be no free choice. Why would anyone do anything wrong if they knew that the Master of the universe was watching intently, judging our deeds, planning our destiny, awaiting our decisions? If we saw the One Above watching us, what merit would there be in virtue?

British researchers have recently found that a picture of eyes is all that's needed to elicit honest behavior. They randomly varied the posters placed over a common lounge honor box where college staff and students would contribute coffee money in the absence of any cashier. When the picture hung above the box was of flowers or a landscape, the coffee money deposited was fairly token, but whenever a picture with eyes was posted there, contributions went up by a factor of three!

Even the *idea* of being watched keeps people honest. How much more is that the case when we realize that there really *is* a consciousness soaking up our actions and calculating the consequences.

The curtain separating Divine knowledge from human awareness grants us freedom and independence, values that we cherish. Abraham knew that freedom is a test, and tradition maintains that he was tested to the hilt. By mastering his mind and heart, he passed his tests, choosing at every opportunity to establish ethical monotheism as the cornerstone of his life.

Gestalt

gestalt (guh-shtält') *n.* - "A configuration or pattern of elements so unified as a whole that its properties cannot be derived from a simple summation of its parts."

Abraham was an ecosystems analyst par excellence. One of ecology's key concepts is that there is a harmony and balance to ecosystems. It's a holistic notion where the whole is greater than the sum of the parts. Abraham, observing nature, recognized that there's more to nature than its parts, and in this way came to recognize the Creator of all.

Birds too see ecosystems. Most songbirds, rather than homing in on one species of tree or shrub, will respond to the overall look of a habitat consisting of many different vegetation variables, like tree size, structure, canopy cover, shrub density, ground cover, and distance to the woodland edge. In short they form a gestalt, or overall impression, something quite separate from this or that detail.

We are and are not like the birds. A bird sees a nature-gestalt and understands whether it's a place to make its home.

Abraham saw a nature-gestalt, and recognizing the unity behind it, resolved to make it a home for its Creator.

G-d is a Verb

Is creation a historical event — or a current one? Scientists have lately discovered "vacuum fluctuations" where matter is continuously coming to be. In chassidic terms it's known for centuries as continuous creation, a process of constant renewal.

Ask your average Josephine on the street, "What is G-d?" and almost certainly you will get some kind of a noun for an answer. Creator, Judge, Merciful One. He, She, It. That's all fine but it's missing something fundamental — action — and logically speaking, that's necessary and we will soon see why.

If we rewind the universe to just before the beginning, we get G-d alone. Fast forward a moment and we get G-d and a universe. The question is this: Where did He put it?

Until He made space, there was no space — there was only Him — alone, complete, unique. That being the case whatever He made was made out of Himself!

This implies that everything else is a dependent reality, while He is the independent reality, the True Reality that underlies all. It is like dreaming or visualizing something.

As long as the mind is on it, it is there. Once attention is removed, it vanishes, just the dreamer is left.

The upshot of all this is that creation is a dynamic process that needs to be continuously renewed, not some one-time prehistoric Event that set the billiard ball universe bouncing at some time in the foggy, distant past. Rather, Creation is here and now.

Once we see G-d as a creative dynamic within the flow of time, the whole concept comes to life. The waves on the beach, birth and death, seasons and songs, all take on a divine quality.

Just meditating on creation *ex nihilo*, something form nothing, *Yesh me'Ayin*, is enough to awaken a sense of the continuous flow of divine energy at every time and place. It seems that Abraham was able to figure this out, and his conclusions were later confirmed by the revelations he received, as recorded in the Torah.

Of the many names by which G-d is known in the Hebrew Bible, the most essential name is the one associated with time. In English, this name is translated as "The Eternal" which has a static implication, like the earth under your feet. But in the original Hebrew, this name is a verb, a dynamic, referring to all of existence continuously coming into being ex nihilo, from nothing to something. The very letters of that Hebrew name, /Yud/, /heh/, /vav/ and /heh/, spell out four forms of the verb to be: Was, is, will be, and continuous coming to be.

This is the notion of G-d being above time, within time, creating time at all times.

Today we have an advantage over the ancients. When they tried to envision continuous creation of diverse beings from a single source, they had to think hard, meditate, and imagine things totally outside their range of experience. Not so you and me. We have modern technology to provide vivid analogies of how continuous creation works.

For instance, a tv image of a tree, as static as it looks, is being refreshed by a new set of scanning electrons some 30 to 60 times per second. It's a new picture every moment. That was Abraham's view of reality as well, a new world every moment. And in recent years, physics has come to accept this view of reality as well.

Bringing creation out of the dusty past and projecting it into the eternal now is about as radical a shift in thinking as you could get. Suddenly the Creator was no longer the great-grandfather god who politely exited the universe for bigger and better things after so kindly fashioning it in the first place. Instead of just being reverently acknowledged as a prehistoric First Cause, the Creator is now seen as an intimately present Current Event.

In a world of change, yes He is the constant. But also the change.

The Present

History is a mystery.
The future is unknown.
Today is a gift.
That's why it's called
The present.

Do you recall your elementary school teacher taking attendance? She'd call your name and you would have to call back, "Present." That meant you were there. There in space, there in time. That was you, nobody else.

Not that we thought about it much back then, but we should be so appreciative about that little fact called existence, being present. There are plenty of things a person can do, but make himself exist is not one of them. Somebody else needs credit for that.

Regardless of whether or not yesterday ever really happened or tomorrow ever will, you still have your today. You've been given existence right now. And now. And now.

Applying the Abraham Principle leads us to continuous creation and that includes continuous creation of you. What an astounding thought! That great big, amazing, all powerful, all knowing, omnipresent First Cause not only notices the likes of a pipsqueak like you, but decides that you're not so bad after all, because having seen all your frailties and weaknesses, he still decided to create you again. And again. And again.

Does that mean that your existence has meaning and purpose? To Somebody, yes. Continuous creation means G-d cares... about you. Because why else would he bother to make you out of nothing at all unless there was some Divine purpose in it. What that purpose is, is another question. But if your whole body, with all its organs and cells and molecules and atoms, were not important, why would you be emerging in full regalia from something to nothing right now? And now? And now?

The previous moment of my existence does not force the next moment's existence any more than the previous moment's image on a TV screen forces the next moment's repeat of the same image. It's there because it was programmed to be there. It was conceived and produced and directed and recorded and encoded and then broadcast and received and decoded and now it's pumping pulses of infinitesimal electrons racing across the screen recreating far away scenes with a refresh rate faster than any eye can detect.

My existence is a byproduct of a process I cannot see. We will 'see' later how and why that's the case, but for now suffice it to say that the process is not visible to the eye. The mind's eye could envision the process but not the physical eye. This invisible code, like the algorithm that informs the TV image, is the information content of reality, or in the language of kabbalah, the Word of G-d.

And in the next Chapter, a Word from our Sponsor.

Walking the Talk

Abraham was a master of insight and rationality. But all the philosophy in the world isn't worth a hill of beans unless you're as ready to walk the walk as much as talk the talk.

Abraham took inventory, but not in the usual sense.

He reviewed all those hard-won ideas he had come to realize by thinking about nature and whatever is beyond it that makes it tick, viz:

- Things don't make themselves; they work by cause and effect.
- Nature is orderly and intelligible; so its ultimate cause must too contain organization and intelligence within it.
- Causes are external to their effects and have power over them; the world's cause must be some external, greater power.
- The cause-and-effect process itself depends on some First Cause.
- All bodies are limited. The First Cause, being unlimited, must not be a body or a form.

- Being unlimited, the First Cause must be equally present both beyond and within the world.
- If this Big Being* (BB) is here and I am too, then He is somehow hiding right here.
- The BB's presence is hidden so we feel independent.
- This impression of independence grants us free will.
- Free will and the ability to think abstractly enable us to 'discover' the BB.
- This 'BB discoverability' is itself a creation, begging the question of why it exists.
- The BB gave us intelligence, independence, free will and the ability to discover Him so that we would exercise those capacities to do just that.
- Consciously living with the BB is the purpose of mankind.

Wow.

Imagine all humanity contemplating the greatness of G-d together. How would the Creator react to such a scenario? It seems only reasonable to believe that He would say to Him/Her/It-self: "Wow. They did it. I hid and they found me. I guess it's time to come out of hiding

---

* Not to be confused with the Big Bang, the Big Being, being the being that banged the Big Bang, assuming for the time being that the Big Bang bung.

and reveal My presence to the whole world while not overwhelming them out of existence."

Until here he got with brain power. From here on in, it's something else. All the philosophy in the world isn't worth a hill of beans unless you're as ready to walk the walk as much as talk the talk. Abraham understood this, as indeed we all should.

To exemplify this, we fast forward to a story of a chassidic master who was visited by two colleagues that were to stay the night in his home. Upon their arrival, he summoned his son and told him to prepare a davar Torah (literally 'word of Torah', a lesson in its teachings) on the subject of honoring guests. The boy took his leave while the men discussed matters and some time later returned to the room.

"What did you prepare?" his father asked. Without a word, the child motioned the men to follow him through the house to guest rooms where beds were freshly made and the customary washbasins and towels were set up in preparation for their stay.

"What do you think?" the father asked his guests. "Is this not an excellent davar Torah on the subject of welcoming guests?"

In any case, what faced Abraham at this point was a life-defining decision. Do I take this mandate wholeheartedly and dedicate the rest of my life on this world to promoting the knowledge of G-d to each and every person I encounter, or not? It's a tough world out there, a world dominated by idolatry, violence, bluff, and power-tripping. Why not just be happy that I found a little truth and meaning for myself and my family? Live and let live. No need to be a fanatic, and go around bursting everyone's bubble, even if those bubbles are as meaningless as they are hollow.

Abraham was one. The world, millions. What hope did he have of making any impact at all? He wasn't rich or powerful and he had no media contacts or PR agencies working for him. And he wasn't even selling anything that tastes good, looks pretty, or fixes your wagon wheel. Plus there was no resale value. Whatever friends he did have must have all given him the same message. Chill. There's no point burning yourself out trying to save the world. Just take care of number one.

So he did. But he decided to take care of Number One, rather than number one. He figured its up to Number One to take care of number one so that number one could take care of Number One.

In short Abraham chose the first option. Live a purposeful life. Spread the word. Share the wisdom. Bring people together in the knowledge of G-d.

A daunting task to be sure, but Abraham was up to it. And since there was a will, he would surely find a way.

Give and Take

Life is full of give and get, but what is our focus? Do we give in order to get? Or get in order to give?

Abraham was a giver. Whatever he had, he shared. So when it came to the things he valued most, his hard earned truths about the existence of G-d and the importance of acknowledging Him, his sharing knew no bounds.

As a child, his father had him help in the family business, the sale of idols. Of course, Abraham had no use for such foolishness but being a dutiful son, he brought the merchandise to market.

Ostensibly hawking his wares, the youth cried out, "Who wants a useless statue that cannot help anyone?" Obviously business was not brisk on the days he worked, but even when customers came of their own accord he dissuaded them. "Madam, you are an elderly woman and this idol was made only yesterday. How could it have power over the world and your life?" "Good thinking lad, thank you." And so it went throughout the day. Predictably, upon returning home with all his stock and no cash, dad was not thrilled, but for Abraham, truth was an asset not to be sold.

As Abraham aged, his priorities did not change, although his methods did. Upon arriving in the Promised Land, he set up a free hostel in the midst of the Negev desert, not exactly the most hospitable of environments. Soon all the nomads and caravan drivers were stopping by because the welcome was warm, the lodgings superb, and the menu lavish. Despite the arid desolation all around, Abraham's table always featured the best delicacies including dairy, baked goods, meat, wine and fruits, all in abundance for anyone who happened by.

When his guests would rise to bless him, Abraham would respond, "Do you think the food was mine? Thank the true owner, the one G-d, Creator of heaven and earth." If they thanked the Creator for the food, the meal was on the house, but if not, he would present them with an itemized bill for hundreds of shekels. "How can things cost so much?" they would ask. But Abraham's reply was irrefutable. "Where else will you find meat, wine and all delicacies in a desert wilderness? Of course it's expensive. But if you will praise the Almighty, it's yours for free."

But rarely would he have to resort to billing. Typically it was enough to share his reasoning. He explained the error of believing that the Creator abandoned the cosmos and relegated its control to various forces. He explained how things don't make themselves and that Divine creation is not like man's. When people create things, they just alter the form. Divine creation is something from nothing and as such, requires constant investment of creative energy. It all made sense to them and they said Grace happily.

But why did he go through all the hassle? If the point was to teach, why bother with an inn, with lodgings, with cuisine and all the work and expense it entailed? Wouldn't public lectures achieve the same result, maybe even better?

But Abraham knew his customers. Not everyone is an intellectual. Just as the human head comprises about 7% of the body's mass, so too brainy types make up about 7% of the body of humanity. That leaves a whole lot of people that need a connect to G-d at a totally different level.

They say the way to a man's heart is through his stomach and I bet women are no different (Chocolates, anyone?). Abraham fed the people, spent his hard-earned money for the physical well-being and comfort of absolute strangers, and then shared all kinds of theological, philosophical and common-sense insights with them as if they were all old college chums. Those that understood accepted it at that level. Those that didn't, resonated with his passion and sincerity and appreciated his love and care. A

G-d of love is a G-d people can relate to and that was the G-d of Abraham.

His gift of monotheism was given from the heart. And the proof was in the pudding.

Ref: Sefer Maamarim — Rebbe Rayyatz — Vayera 5701.

Knowing and Caring

Go out on the street and ask your average Al, "What's your opinion about ignorance and apathy?" And your average answer? "I don't know and I don't care."

To know and to care. That was the life of Abraham.

Discovering ultimate reality was his driving passion; he stopped at nothing short of absolute truth. But as perfectly noble as that is, it was not good enough. Abraham wanted to share – with everyone.

His goal – the whole world knowing and celebrating one G-d. His problem – Most people just weren't interested. Are things any different today?

Go out on the street and ask your average George, "What's your opinion about ignorance and apathy?" And your average answer? "I don't know and I don't care."

Abraham was ultimately successful re-engineering the public mind, but even his successes may have felt a little hollow, because after all, where was G-d in this whole picture? True, He was the ultimate reality of everything, making nature tick and all. But he remained unheard and unseen, theoretical.

Why didn't He reveal Himself? If the purpose was to be discovered, and we discover Him, and even share that discovery, then what? Shouldn't He come out of hiding and say Voila! Here I am!?

In a way, that is what happened. But just in a way. The Midrash relates the story of the Divine response to Abraham's quest with the following parable:

"And G-d said to Abraham: 'Go from your land, your birthplace, and your father's house…'" (Genesis 12:2) — To what may this be compared? To a man who was traveling from place to place when he saw a palace in flames. He wondered: "Is it possible that the palace has no owner?" The owner of the palace looked out and said, "I am the owner of the palace." So Abraham our father said, "Is it possible that the world lacks a ruler?" G-d looked out and said to him, "I am the ruler, the Sovereign of the universe."

We can readily appreciate why Abraham was perplexed. This sensitive human being gazes at a brilliantly structured universe, a splendid piece of art. He is overwhelmed by the grandeur of a sunset and by the miracle of childbirth; he marvels at the roaring ocean waves and at the silent, steady beat of the human heart. The world is indeed a palace.

But the palace is in flames. The world is full of bloodshed, injustice and strife. Thugs, abusers, rapists, kidnappers and killers are continuously demolishing the palace, turning our world into an ugly tragic battlefield of untold pain and horror.

What happened to the owner of the palace? Abraham cries. Why does G-d allow man to destroy His world? Why does He permit such a beautiful palace to go up in flames? Could G-d have made a world only to abandon it? Would anyone build a palace and then desert it?

The Midrash records G-d's reply: "The owner of the palace looked out and said: 'I am the owner of the palace.' G-d looked out and said to Abraham: 'I am the ruler, the Sovereign of the universe.'"

What is the meaning of G-d's response?

Note that the owner of the palace does not make an attempt to get out of the burning building or to extinguish the flames. He is merely stating that He is the owner of the palace that is going up in smoke. It is as if, instead of racing out, the owner were calling for help. G-d made the palace, man set it on fire, and only man can put out the flames. Abraham asks G-d, "Where are you?" G-d replies, "I am here, where are you?" Man asks G-d, "Why did You abandon the world?" G-d asks man, "Why did you abandon Me?"

Thus began the revolution of Judaism — humanity's courageous venture to extinguish the flames of immorality and bloodshed and restore the world to the harmonious and sacred palace it was intended to be. Abraham's encounter with G-d in the presence of a burning palace gave birth to the mission statement of Judaism – to negate evil and assert good, making the palace fit for a King, and all his subjects, too.

(Ref's: Midrash Rabbah Bereishit 39:1; based on an interpretation by R' Jonathan Sacks in Radical Then, Radical Now, Harper Collins, 2000, and the linked article citing it by R' Yossi Jacobson on Chabad.org).

Beauty, Meet Truth

Abraham's style was beautiful, but he didn't stop there. His commitment went far beyond his natural goodness, far beyond his kind and wise nature. His commitment was ultimate, and that can look scary... very scary.

I am not a Kabbalist. Nor a philosopher.

If I were, I could speak of sublime realities like beauty and truth in something approaching an authoritative fashion. But all I can muster is a few life lessons and some Torah gleanings.

For instance. Sometimes truth is ugly.

Take Abraham for example. Here is a man who is everybody's hero. Who else could be adored by Christian, Muslim and Jew? Founder of ethical monotheism, host par excellence, educator, iconoclast, at once challenging men to rise above their mediocrity, yet challenging G-d to descend from His uncompromising excellence and value us for who we are.

Yes, Abraham was beautiful, but he didn't stop there. His commitment went far beyond his natural goodness, far beyond his kind and wise nature. His commitment was ultimate, and that can look scary, very scary.

Abraham's biggest test, the binding of Isaac, is not the kind of deed one calls wise, or kind, or sane for that matter. I recall studying the Akeida, the story of the binding of Isaac, with a brilliant scholar who loved nothing more than Torah. But this story bugged him, no, actually haunted him. "He was wrong! He had no right to do it!" The story drove him nuts. Here's why.

Abraham built his entire life on promoting G-d in the world. He weaned the Middle East off of idolatry, taught people, fed them, nurtured their faith in an all-knowing, just and benevolent Creator. He was a living model of the good G-d about Whom he preached.

Then came his big test: To offer up Isaac as a sacrifice. Which sounds a lot like this: Commit murder. Kill a human being. Kill your own son. Your only son. The one you love. The promised father-to-be of your millions of children. Go ahead. Make me a liar. Tie him up and slit his throat. Watch him bleed to death. Trash your life, trash My reputation, and don't ask why. Just do it.

Well, you may recall, in the end it wasn't so bad. At the last moment, G-d said "Stop". He just wanted the offer, not the deed. Yes, G-d was beautiful, but Abraham did not want to stop there. "Let me take just a drop of blood." Even then, Abraham was ready to serve in truth, ultimate truth. And that ain't pretty.

But then again, I'm not a philosopher, nor a Kabbalist.

If I were, I might see the beauty within the ugliness, the virtue of sacrificing a beloved child. But guess what. I can't. All I know is "G-d said so." And in truth, that's enough.

If the eyes of the beholder belong to G-d, it just may be that truth is beautiful. If I had His eyes, I'd think so too. But I'm standing too close to the brushstrokes, and that crimson rose petal looks like a drop of blood to me.

Truth be Told: Stories

The colleagues of the Alter Rebbe, Rabbi Shneur Zalman of Liadi, once had a discussion about how each of them would run the world if he were G-d, each offering their opinions on how things could be improved upon. When they were done, the Alter Rebbe said his piece. "If I were G-d, I'd do things just the same as He does them."

This same Alter Rebbe wrote the primary resource for Chassidic philosophy, the Tanya, and in it enshrines service in truth as the Jewish way. The present Rebbe writes that if he would have left that out of the Tanya, he would have had another 50,000 followers. But truth is not for sale.

I've checked my toolkit for a nice big yardstick and I haven't yet found one big enough to measure G-d's beauty, nor his truth for that matter. But is it He that must pass my tests?

My mother, may she live and be well, rarely speaks of her war experiences, so when, as a child, she chose to share with me a lesson from the Lodz ghetto, it made a lasting impression. What got her going was me telling her exactly what I would do if there were a fire at that moment. She said, "Don't be silly. You don't know what you would do in a big test like that."

"When I was in ghetto," she continued, "Two men were arrested by the Nazis for the 'crime' of possessing a radio. Before they were hauled off for interrogation as to who else could be implicated, the younger of the two, a strong, handsome young man said, 'Let them do what they will, they'll never get any information out of me!' The elder detainee said nothing. He was old and wizened, and looked like you could blow him over.

"That very afternoon, the burly youth returned having told everything he knew about everyone with a radio, just under the threat of torture. The elderly Jew returned only three days later, his fingernails pulled off and his eyes gouged out.

"So," concluded my mom, "Don't say you know what you will do under a test, because you just don't know."

Who is more beautiful? The strong, handsome youth who spoke? Or the, blinded and maimed old man who didn't?

Life is not simple.

But let's put it into terms that a child could understand. The teacher turns his back on the class and a bunch of kids act up, making lots of trouble. Most of the class starts giggling. Things get out of control. After his call for order falls on deaf ears, the teacher calls out, "That's it, class detention. No recess today."

"Whoa! Why? That's not fair! I didn't do it! It was him! Why should I get in trouble for something I didn't do? Why should I behave good? I see it just gets me into trouble."

"I'm sorry class, but I've told you many times. We are all in this together. We all have a responsibility, and if the class can't move forward, you have to make up the time."

Life is not fair, at least not to our standards of fair. But if we recognize where our knocks are coming from, we will take them with humility. If it's from G-d, it's good. Does that make it beautiful? In truth, yes. But in our eyes?

We Jews are an interesting lot. We are proud of our faith despite the bitter exiles, the terrible pogroms, the unspeakable evils of the Inquisition, the Holocaust, and the mess we are in today. Yet as soon as it touches us personally, there are questions.

One last story. I heard it at an event marking the first anniversary of passing of a wonderful young man who was killed by a train in a freak accident. He had been on his way to synagogue to help make up a quorum for communal prayer. That young man was my son's Grade 5 teacher, every kid's favorite teacher, the kindest person you'd ever care to meet. R' Yosi Jacobson spoke at the memorial and shared this story with the huge crowd gathered there.

There was a Chassidic lumber merchant over a century ago, who was famous for two things. Loads of cash and unstinting support of Torah study in his town. He funded an entire study hall of bright and dedicated Torah scholars and whenever he could, he would join with them in exploring the truth and beauty of the Torah.

One year he had a great idea. Instead of buying one boatload of lumber, he'd buy three, so when he sold it, he'd make lots more money and be able to do so many more good deeds with the charity he could spend. He spent all his savings on this grand project, and once the three ships were laden and sailing off to their foreign markets, he happily settled back into his satisfying communal and spiritual life.

But not for long. One of the local Torah scholars got wind of the storm first. The boats had all capsized. All the lumber was lost. Their gracious benefactor was ruined, but he didn't know it yet. Who would break the terrible news? And how?

Finally one young man agreed to shoulder the painful task. He conferred with his colleagues, planned his pitch and went off to see the lumber merchant at his home. "I have a question on a difficult piece of Talmud. Can you help me?"

"Me? Help you? I doubt if I can solve something you don't know, but since you're here, let's give it a try. You know I'd help you any way I can."

"Well, it says over here that we are obliged to bless G-d for the bad, exactly as we bless him for good? How is that possible?"

"That's your question?" asked the merchant. "Well, I'm no expert in Talmud but I think I can help you on this one.

You see everything comes from G-d, so when bad things happen, they aren't really bad. They just seem bad to us because we have a very limited point of view. G-d has a big plan for everything, so knowing this we can feel secure and even happy that this apparent bad is deep down positive, and G-d is really doing us a favor by treating us in this way. Do you get it?"

"Well, yes and no. I understand and believe that it's all for the best and all, but my difficulty is being just as happy about bad news as good. I mean, picture this. Say you married off a child and you were at the wedding. Would you dance from joy?"

"Of course I would! Who wouldn't?"

"And if all your boats loaded with lumber were to capsize en route to market leaving you penniless, crushed in debt, and without means to climb out of it, would you dance from joy?"

"Uh… dance from joy? Well, uh… I see what you're getting at. But if you think about it, the One Above knows what's best for us and he has our good at heart. In fact when things turn out bad in our eyes it's actually a sign that the goodness within is much greater than a revealed good. It's all explained in Chassidus."

"Yes but would you dance?"

"If all my ships suddenly capsized leaving me flat broke and in debt up to my eyeballs? Well, yeah.. ..yeah. I wouldn't normally think about it in those terms, but now that I am, yes I guess I would dance."

"Just as much as at the wedding of your own child?"

"Yes! Yes! Just as much, and maybe even more!"

"Well, start dancing. There really was a storm at sea. A messenger came to the study hall and told us. I verified the story myself and it's true. All your lumber has been lost."

The merchant fainted on the spot. When he came to, he said, "You know, at this moment, I'm having trouble with that Talmudic passage myself!"

The "Why" Chromosome

> *Faith and reason are not really like trains in collision — they are more like trains in series: One picks up where the other leaves off.*

Kids are weird. All the stuff that we clever, worldly grown-ups so sensibly take for granted, children question. Which parent has not fielded such curve-ball queries as:

"Why is the sky blue?"

"Why does daddy have a moustache and you don't?"

"Why do people die?"

You stop and think. You wonder at her wondering, take pride in her cleverness, and dig deep into the recesses of your mind to dredge up some long- forgotten explanation. Thinking how best to say it, you repackage the idea, trim off some details, choose easy words, and tell it like it is, expecting (naively) that your kid will be satisfied and the matter happily laid to rest.

"The sky is blue because the air scatters around the other colors but lets the blue through."

"Daddy has a moustache because men have a chemical in their blood called testosterone that makes facial hair grow."

"People die because their bodies wear out."

So the kid soaks it up, ponders a bit, rolls his toy car, pats her doll, runs a bit around the room and off you go back to your things, thinking the case is closed until one or two hours or days later when you face the next round of reality checking.

"But why doesn't the air scatter the blue light?"

"Why don't you have testosterone?"

"Why do bodies wear out?"

Usually not, but sometimes the questioning turns into a game called Let's-Keep-Mommy-Talking-as-Long-as-Possible-by-Asking-an-Endless-Series-of-Why's. But even then, a sincere childish curiosity underlies the game, a need to know the explanation of things.

Of course the game is not restricted to children. The fact that most of us outgrow our inherent curiosity about the world is not so much because we know the answers but more because as life grinds on, we become dulled to the wondrous workings of the world around us. By the time we hit our age, the only "why" most of us ask is "why me?" Most of us except scientists of course.

Maybe scientists are more sensitive. Maybe they just never grew up. Or maybe it's an overactive Why Chromosome on their DNA. Whatever it is, the question remains: Why the Why?

Answering this turns out to be more important than it looks at first, because the uniquely human habit of seeking explanations drives two of the most powerful social forces at work today: science and religion. And since the two seem all too often at loggerheads, it may be worth the effort to investigate how one little question can generate two such radically different answers.

As with many other questions, we can use the Abraham Principle to resolve this too. The Abraham Principle asserts that when two entities comprise one system, this correlation itself implies the existence of some third being or causal force, external to and more powerful than them, which determines their form or mode of behavior.

For the scientist, the question 'why' is a journey from effect to cause and getting there is half the fun. The other half is knowing that regardless of what we discover, the original questions somehow remain while new questions abound. For the sincerely religious also, the question 'why' is an exploration, but one that ends not with some infinite regress, nor endless stream of questions, but rather with an ultimate answer: That there is a First Cause that seeded the world, planted the 'why chromosome' in our psyches, and gave us the logical prowess to infer back to the source, the ultimate Because before which there is no why. And why would He do a thing like that? Well, why not?

The Power of One

There are those who have no use for things simple, invisible, unknowable — until it's time to flick the switch! Electrifying.

Unity is simplicity.

How easy it is to say, how elusive to grasp. Yet precisely this is the heritage of Abraham. His notion of a simple unity underlying everything can be better understood with a modern analogy — electricity. Electricity, too, is an invisible reality, hidden behind the walls, yet turning everything on, lightbulbs and lawn mowers, ovens and clocks, making the world tick.

But all this is just what it does. What is electricity, really, in and of itself, before we flick the switch? Descriptions abound. The first ten sources on dictionary.com have definitions ranging all over the map. But what we all can agree on is that there is a potential energy stored in those wires that can do any number of things once released. Moreover, the uses we put electricity to don't change the electricity itself. Electricity remains quite independent of its various actions even when powering many functions in many places at once.

Perhaps we can say the same of G-d. The Abraham Principle leads us to a First Being upon which everything depends.* One of the implications of being First is being independent. Everything needs it but it doesn't need anything. Because think about it. If the First Being was conditional on something else, then that something would be the First. So however you slice it, the First Being is an independent entity.

Independence is not something you share. It sets you apart, alone. So there's no such thing as "tied for first place" in the race for an ultimate solution to the problem of existence. And the closer we look at the gold medallist, the less He looks like the silver or the bronze. Unlike His competitors, He has no legs, no body, not even a head. G-d is not organic, nor composite. His unity is simple.

---

* Even if, for argument's sake, you wanted to say that there is no First Being but that cause-and-effect go on eternally, you could still look at that eternal cause-and-effect system and ask why it exists. A systems analytic approach will ultimately yield a simple unity on which the whole is predicated.

Alternatively one may argue that instead of a First Being, there are two (or more) first beings and they are co-dependent, not independent. If so, then again the Abraham Principle will query the order of the two-being system, and determine that there must be a third entity, external to and more powerful than these that integrates their functioning. The result? An independent First Being.

Perfectly simple. And that makes Him look like a loser. Looks like. For He is not only *a* winner. He's *the* winner.

See that wall? The electrons are there, in the wires behind it, incredibly powerful, waiting to fulfill every potential. The full force of Niagara Falls plus a continent's worth of thermonuclear grid is behind that wall, quiet, unseen.

The fool says, "Nah." The wise man plugs in and flicks the switch. Or sometimes it's the philosopher that says "Nah" and the simple person who plugs in and flicks the switch. You don't have to be an electrical engineer to run a dishwasher, and you don't need to be theologian to do a mitzvah. We are all plugged in to the source. We just have to flick the switch and the light goes on.

Better than solar, when you run on divine energy, you never run out. It's the ultimate renewable. No matter that it's undefined. Don't worry that it's invisible. You've got what it takes – the hardware, the operator's manual, and an extended lifetime warranty – rechargeable batteries included.

Ref's - Abarbanel, Rosh Amanah, Ch. 7, and Tzemach Tzedek, Derech Mitzvotecha, p.45A.

What is Life?

A simple yet elusive quest for an answer takes us from biology to kabbalah to the dance of the electron.

If a biologist knows about anything at all, he should know about life. Or so you would think. After all, biology is defined as the scientific study of living organisms. To distinguish biology from other scholarly disciplines, introductory textbooks tackle the terms of engagement right from the start. Typically on page 1, they take their own run at that classic, primordial question that has stymied philosophers since the dawn of civilization and that is: What is life?

Defining life is particularly daunting because it is a fundamental concept, rather like 'time' or 'consciousness'. Each of these is a basic reality that doesn't break down into parts. As such, the exercise of defining life leads us between a rock and a hard place. On the one hand, you can't define life in terms of itself, for that would be trivial. On the other hand, once you characterize it with a shopping list of descriptors, you've completely lost its essence.

What to do? Probably not what the experts do. Biologists, locked as they are in the outdated materialistic mindsets of the 19th Century, try to define something fuzzy like life in terms of rocks and hard places. "Life is the characteristic quality of living beings." or "Life is defined by such features as homeostasis, metabolism, reproduction, mobility, and genetic makeup."

It sounds okay for starters, but scratch the surface of these 'definitive' statements and the former is just a tautology (self-reference), while the latter is an elliptical trajectory around the missing focal point. Besides, do those qualities really distinguish living beings from others? Let's take a look at a few.

Homeostasis is the maintenance of a constant internal environment by means of negative feedback. This means that if it's too hot, you sweat and bring down the body temperature. Too cold? You shiver and warm up. That's life. But what about my furnace, thermometer and thermostat? That's a homeostatic system too! Too hot? The thermometer signals the thermostat to shut down the furnace. Too cold? The thermometer signals the thermostat to turn the heat back on. Voila! Thermoregulation, i.e., homeostasis, a constant internal environment. Does that mean my house is alive? Obviously not.

The same is true of the other 'defining' qualities of life. Crystals, too, reproduce. Automobiles can be said to metabolize. And viruses, which are considered nonliving, are comprised of genetic material just as living cells are.

So what is life?

To discover what life is, let's probe the animal. The word animal is derived from the Latin, animus, meaning mind or soul, which is similar to the Latin anima, for breath or spirit. Hebrew also speaks of neshama and neshima, which are soul and breath, respectively. As well we have the related ruach, which is both spirit and wind. Similarly the English word inspiration refers both to physical breath and spiritual arousal.

A person that is animated, that has vitality, life, is recognizable by a dynamic presence, a spiritual investment that is quite beyond the physical yet expresses itself specifically through his body and its functions. It is an enigmatic fact of life that we recognize the transcendence of life itself by observing its investment in the physical bodies of living beings.

But how do these two worlds mesh? What is it that unites and harmonizes the nonphysical spirit with the corporeal body? Neither the body itself, nor the spirit alone, have the capacity to effect the integrated soul-body unity of a living being.

There must be something beyond both soul and body that creates them with the potential for unification and combines them as an organic unit. This is the logic of the Abraham Principle, and through it, the venerable patriarch determined that there is but a singular source of life, the First Being, whose Life is independent of both body and soul.

It is in celebration of this wonderful reality, that Jews begin each day with a prayer immediately upon waking up in the morning, saying, "I offer thanks to you, living and eternal King, for You have mercifully restored my soul within me; Your faithfulness is great."

Loosely translated, Modeh Ani means, "Hey! I've got this body and this soul that really have nothing to do with each other. It's just that some great Being beyond them both has made them and put them together so I can celebrate life itself. Thank you!"

We then go on to acknowledge all the details of how that essential life is expressed in day-to-day existence. We have blessings for daybreak, for vision, for movement, for strength, for clothing, for identity and for freedom. But heading this long list of blessings is one for life.

"My G-d, the soul which You have given within me is pure. You have created it, You have formed it, You have breathed it into me, and You preserve it within me. You will eventually take it from me, and restore it within me in the Time to Come. So long as the soul is within me, I offer thanks to You, L-rd, my G-d and G-d of my fathers, Master of all works, L-rd of all souls. Blessed are You, L-rd, who restores souls to dead bodies."

Chassidus explains this prayer in terms of the Kabbalah of Life. The stages of the soul's descent into the physical world are described above as 'pure', 'created', 'formed', 'breathed', and 'preserved'. The first four terms refer to its stepwise descent through the four spiritual worlds of Atzilut-emanation (pure), Beriyah-creation (created), Yetsira-formation (formed), and Asiyah-action (breathed). The fifth is the continuous miracle of sustained physical life (preserved). Before each term, the word Atah-You is used, indicating that G-d Himself, the Creator of something from nothing, is behind each quantum jump from world to world and is continuously involved in sustaining the soul-body unity.

If this sounds esoteric to you, don't worry – it is. But as it turns out, physical reality is just as strange, for particle physics provides a close analogy to this spiritual odyssey, and does so in the name of the ubiquitous electron. Indeed, quantum jumps within the atom lend credence to the sentiment that Adam and the atom have enough in common to warrant similar names.

Strange as it seems, when electrons move from level to level in their atomic orbits, they do so without covering the intervening space. Unlike larger objects that at least seem to obey classical laws of continuous motion, the electron jumps in a most radical fashion. It instantaneously changes state, so at the very same moment, it vanishes from one location and reappears in another. Moreover the electron not only jumps from place to place, but also from time to time and from energy level to energy level, all without ever traversing intermediate conditions.

In like fashion, these "soul-jumps" from world to world also occur in a marvelous, something-from-nothing manner which mirrors the mysterious leaps of the electron from level to level. On the other side of the mirror, in the spiritual realm, the Atah-power behind the soul's quantum descents is called Atzmut-essence. This essence is the indivisible wholeness that is the ultimate reality of the world, putting it all together without being seen.

So too in the 'life' of the electron. Every electron leap is an expression of an indivisible wholeness, a creative force beyond space and time, which is the ultimate ground of reality, is conscious, and manifests in each and every particle in the cosmos, putting it all together without being seen.

It is here that faith and physics kiss. The life of the Adam and the life of the atom are one and the same, an unutterable essence that cannot be perceived directly but is somehow recognizable in every step in the dance of life, a dance that continues into the Days of Moshiach when the world will be filled with the knowledge of G-d as the waters cover the sea.

(Inspired by a talk of the Lubavitcher Rebbe dated 16 Teves 5750.)

Faith and Physics: A Story

Back in the spring of 1987, I was called aside one morning by Rabbi Dovid Schochet, the senior Rabbi of the Lubavitch community in Toronto, with an odd request:

"You should get a copy of this month's Reader's Digest. There is an article about a physicist, John Wheeler. You should get in touch with him."

"But what should I tell him?"

"Share with him some Chassidus (chassidic teaching), the Seven Noahide Laws, that kind of thing."

My curiosity was piqued. Rabbi Schochet is a man who lives and breathes Torah from morning until night. Yet apparently not only does he read Reader's Digest, he is using it to single out a non-Jewish scientist to get close with. But once I read the article, it started to make sense.

Wheeler was one of the world's leading physicists. At the time, he was putting out some very religious sounding statements in the name of hard-nosed science. "Is man an unimportant bit of dust on an unimportant planet in an unimportant galaxy somewhere in the vastness of space?" asks Wheeler. "No! The necessity to produce life lies at the centre of the universe's whole machinery and design... Without an observer, there are no laws of physics... Why should the universe exist at all? The explanation must be so simple and so beautiful that when we see it we will all say, 'How could it have been otherwise?...' Still needed today is a thinker... who can lead the way surefootedly through this world of mystery to insights overlooked or deemed impossible. I don't know how to. I don't know anyone who does. I can only say that when you see one who does, treasure him or her."

Here we have a scientist is reporting the discovery of a supernatural plan, the centrality of mankind in that plan, and the expectation that some individual will soon lead us to realize the purpose of creation. And all this is the rational conclusion of a physicist who collaborated with Niels Bohr to lay the groundwork for atomic energy, coined the phrase "black hole", and served as mentor for several Nobel laureates. How intriguing!

I drafted a letter to Professor Wheeler and set out to look for where to deliver it. I called Reader's Digest. They couldn't help me. I looked for the author of the article, John Boslough, but I couldn't find him. I checked at the University of Texas at Austin where Professor Wheeler was reportedly working. They hadn't seen him for months. I tried tracking him through Europe and North America, calling a steady stream of other campuses where he had recently been, but no luck.

I decided to call several physicists and put them on the trail. I finally found Wheeler's personal secretary at Princeton. "I'm sorry sir, he's very busy for the next few months... Yes, I understand that your message is very important, but he's just left for his annual retreat to a little island off the coast of Maine and and he's not taking any but the most urgent calls."

"What is he doing there?"

"He's thinking."

"But what is he thinking about?"

"Being and nothingness."

Bingo! Exactly what I needed to reach him about. I packaged up a Tanya, the blueprint of Chassidic philosophy containing several chapters discussing the process and nature of creation ex nihilo. I included a letter explaining a little about the Rebbe, and how Chassidus has the answers to his questions regarding the origin, mechanism and purpose of the continuous creation of "something from nothing."

After sending it off, I called his secretary, petitioning her politely to pass the package on promptly. She replied,

"Dr. Gotfryd, you must understand, around here I must get a dozen manuscripts a week for Professor Wheeler's review and comment, and each one is clearly labeled, 'Don't take the next breath until you've read this!'" Send it if you want, but no guarantees he'll ever see it.

Nevertheless, within a few weeks I received in the mail Wheeler's hand-signed "review" on Princeton Physics Department stationery:

"It is for me a precious remembrance of the life and teachings of the seventh Lubavitcher Rebbe to have as a kind gift from you the Tanya of the first Lubavitcher Rebbe. I thank you especially for marking passages that I might study with especial care. You will already have some notion of my sympathy for these general questions in what I have said or written about creation, for example, in the enclosed three pages of a paper of mine given at a joint meeting of the Royal Society and the American Philosophical Society."

The article he sent me, entitled "Delayed-Choice Experiments", is noteworthy: He points out that the elementary quantum process is an act of creation, the result of observer-participation. From this it follows that without man there is no universe and no laws of physics. Wheeler finds an original allusion to this notion in Midrash Rabbah, a compilation of Talmudic insights into the Torah, which he quotes:

G-d chides Abraham, 'You would not even exist if it were not for me!'

'Yes, G-d, that I know," Abraham replies, 'but You would not be known were it not for me.'

Dr Wheeler comments that, "In our time, the participants in the dialogue have changed. They are the universe and man. The universe, in the words of some who would aspire to speak for it, says, 'I am a giant machine. I supply the space and time for your existence. There was no before before I came into being, and there will be no after after I cease to exist. You are an unimportant bit of matter located in an unimportant galaxy.'"

"How shall we reply? Shall we say, 'Yes, oh universe, without you I would not have been able to come into being. Yet you great system are made of phenomena; and every phenomenon rests on an act of observation. You could never even exist without elementary acts of registration such as mine.'?"

This, in a nutshell, is the Jewish concept that "for my sake was the world created". Humanity was not created as part of the universe. The universe was created for humanity. Such a model requires the necessity of continuous creation, of humanity's unique role and purpose, and of a consciousness underlying the universe as a whole.

It's actually quite poetic. First Abraham finds G-d through science. Then, some 3,700 years later, quantum physics finds G-d through science. And now John Wheeler finds out that Abraham had it right all along.

As to Wheeler's search for a "thinker who can lead the way surefootedly through this world of mystery to insights overlooked or deemed impossible", I have done my small part by introducing the Rebbe and Chabad Chassidism to John Wheeler, with good results. What's left for us all is to follow Wheeler's concluding advice -- "Treasure him."

About the Author

Dr. Arnie Gotfryd, PhD, is an observant Jew, scientist and educator living in Toronto, Canada. He has authored or edited five books and over 300 popular and scholarly articles, has lectured in 40 cities on four continents, and has been featured on television and radio as well. His accredited university course on Faith and Science earned him a Templeton Award of Excellence and for many years drew the largest attendance of any course offered at the University of Toronto's New College in the Faculty of Arts and Sciences.

His community and social service work has included directing programs for at-risk teens and an international adoption agency which has placed over 300 orphans.

Professionally he directs Maxi Mind Learning Centres, Inc. (www.maximind.ca), which uses neuro-educational techniques to train attention-challenged children to focus without medication so they can succeed in learning and in life.